THE EMBLEM
THE ARMS & THE MOTTO
OF THE UNIVERSITY
OF CAMBRIDGE

NOTES
ON THEIR USE BY
UNIVERSITY PRINTERS

THE EMBLEM
THE ARMS & THE MOTTO
OF THE UNIVERSITY
OF CAMBRIDGE

NOTES
ON THEIR USE BY
UNIVERSITY PRINTERS
BY THE

REV. H. P. STOKES
LITT.D.

PRINTED AT
THE UNIVERSITY PRESS
CAMBRIDGE

CAMBRIDGE UNIVERSITY PRESS

Cambridge, New York, Melbourne, Madrid, Cape Town, Singapore,
São Paulo, Delhi, Dubai, Tokyo, Mexico City

Cambridge University Press
The Edinburgh Building, Cambridge CB2 8RU, UK

Published in the United States of America by Cambridge University Press, New York

www.cambridge.org
Information on this title: www.cambridge.org/9780521166355

First published 1928
First paperback edition 2010

A catalogue record for this publication is available from the British Library

ISBN 978-0-521-16635-5 Paperback

LIST OF DEVICES

LIST OF DEVICES (contd)

LIST OF DEVICES (contd)

THE EMBLEM

THE EMBLEM

WHEN the two sumptuous volumes known as *The Cambridge Portfolio* were edited by the Rev. J. J. Smith, of Caius, in the year 1840, one of the most remarkable articles was that on "The Cambridge Press." It was written by young Mr A. J. Beresford Hope, then an undergraduate at Trinity. It contained a detailed account of the University Printers and of their work. Alluding to John Legate, who succeeded Thomas Thomas, M.A., in 1588, it stated that it was he "who first, in the year 1606, adopted the well-known figure of 'Alma Mater Cantabrigiensis,' with the motto 'Hinc lucem et pocula sacra.' We subjoin (it added), for the amusement of the reader two varieties of this emblem—one in sooth rude enough." These are reproduced below (see Nos. 2 and 12).

We propose here to give illustrations of this renowned Cambridge device and legend. But first let it be noted that the date of their use has been thrown back. The late Mr Bowes in his *Biographical Notes on the Printers*, says that John Legate "used the impression *from 1603 onward.*" Later the present writer thought he possessed the earliest issue prefixed to an edition of W. Perkins's *Warning against the Idolatrie of the last times*, dated 1601.

Lately, however, the Free Library in our town has acquired a fine print of the emblem, surrounded by the legend, printed by John Legate in the year 1600 on the title-page of an edition of Perkins's *A Golden Chaine*.

Whether earlier copies will be forthcoming, remains to be seen.

With a reproduction of this (No. 1) we may well begin our illustrations, for it is the largest of all the representations, measuring 97 × 71 mm.

It will be seen that an ornamental oval device has in the centre a pedestal, on the front of which is printed ALMA MATER CANTABRIGIA. From behind the pedestal rises a nude female figure, three-quarter length, with flowing hair, crowned with a mural crown rising out of a wreath. In her left hand she holds a cup or chalice, receiving drops from a cloud; and in her right hand a sun radiated. On each side of the pedestal stands an olive tree; while in the background there is a river, with a sail-boat on one side, and a rowing-boat on the other. Beyond under the sun is a castle, or a church; and under the chalice a town with spires and towers. The whole is surrounded by the motto *Hinc lucem et pocula sacra*.

Next in order of size (67 × 57 mm.) comes No. 2, the representation reproduced in *The Cambridge Port-folio* for the amusement of the reader—a variety of the emblem, "in sooth rude enough," as Mr A. J. Beres-ford Hope remarked. In this rough picture there is no background.

No. 3 is more elegantly drawn. Again there is no background.

It was used by J. Legate in 1601 in Perkins's *Warning against Idolatry*, in Hill's *Life Everlasting*, etc.; in the 7th edition of Thomas's *Dictionary* (1606); and so on.

It was probably taken (see Bowes and McKerrow) by J. Legate the elder to London in 1610; but apparently not used by him there. The younger Legate had it on his father's death in 1620; and it was used by him in 1631 and in 1637.

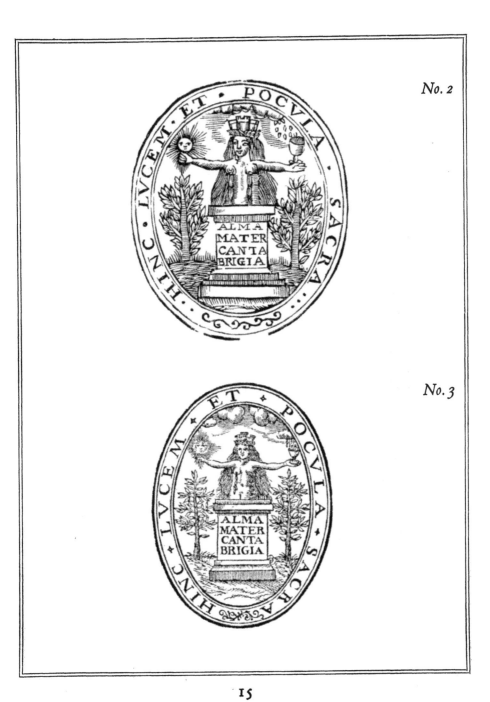

No. 2

No. 3

The next three specimens should, if the bordure be included, perhaps have been treated before the laſt two —as far as size goes. They differ from the preceding in various points: (1) as mentioned above, there is an ornament surrounding the garter (71 × 47 mm.); (2) the legend border begins with the word HINC at the top right hand; (3) the cup is held in the right hand and the radiated sun in the left; (4) the arms are bent upwards, and not held out ſtraight; and (5) poplar trees replace olives on either side.

Nos. 4 and 5 are generally similar; though of different sizes. A specimen of No. 4 is seen in the *Hymenaeus Cantabrigiensis*, published by John Hayes in 1683. The smaller issue may be found in Isaac New﹣ton's edition of the *Geographia Generalis* of Bernhard Varenus, printed at the same office in 1681.

No. 5 measures 45 × 34 mm. including the orna﹣ment; 45 × 30 mm. as to the legend border.

No. 6 is another ornamental oval device (56 × 43 mm.); with the cup in the right hand, and so on. It may be seen in John Field's *Holy Bible*, printed in 1668. The engraved title is by John Chantry, after the design of Robert Vaughan, 1657.

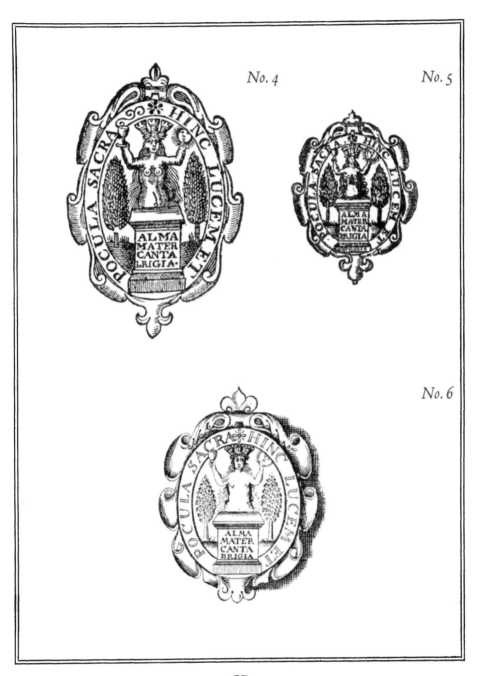

No. 4

No. 5

No. 6

We now come to two designs, earlier in date but smaller in size, which may be treated together on account of their points of similarity, though they differ in various particulars.

The first (No. 7) was issued by John Legate the elder as early as 1601, according to McKerrow, who gives the measurements as 44·5 × 26 mm.; but this breadth is probably a mistake; it should doubtless be 44·5 × 34·5 mm.

Prof. Playfair's sermon, *The Sick-Man's Couch*, was printed in 1605; and a *Tractatus* by Lipsius in 1607; etc. It was probably taken by Legate sen. to London in 1610, and passed to John Legate jun. in 1620. Kellet's *Miscellanies of Divinity* was issued in 1635.

In No. 7, "the cup does not touch the enclosing rule," McKerrow points out; whilst in No. 8 the cup touches the rim. In this latter form of the device—which is later in date—there are also other differences; *e.g.* as to the printing of the legend border; as to the trees; as to the position of the sun, etc.; yet the size is the same (44·5 × 34·5 mm.). Several issues of No. 8 were published by T. and J. Buck from 1629 onwards, and by them and Roger Daniel, who from 1640 issued copies in his name only.

No. 7

No. 8

A group of small-sized emblems may be considered next. Of these Mr Ronald B. McKerrow, in his *Printers' and Publishers' Devices* (1913), speaks of Mr C. Sayle's *Printed Books*:

Mr Sayle, on pp. 1269 and 1286, notes a device of this type measuring 33 mm. and on p. 1284 one measuring 31·5 mm., apparently considering that these differ. There is, indeed, an extraordinary variation in the sizes of prints of the device: I have found it of all heights from 31 to 33·5 mm., but after careful examination of a number of prints, I have failed to discover any evidence that there was more than one block. The differences in size, great as they are, might, I think, be accounted for by the use of different kinds of paper and varying degrees of dampness at the time of the impression.

No. 9, measuring 35 × 27 mm., has on the pedestal AL|MAM|ATER. This is seen in *Quaestio Quodlibetica* printed by the Bucks in 1630; but, in the following year, these capitals were cut out (No. 10), and "Alma Mater" inserted in type in two lines (1631 and following years). The drawing is what Mr Beresford Hope would call "rude enough."

No. 9

No. 10

Later we find—as we still find—impressions from blocks of the same convenient size, with the words ALMA MATER CANTABRIGIA in four lines on the pedestal. The legend is printed in differing types (see Nos. 11, 12 and 13). No. 11 is from *The University Calendar* of 1809, No. 12 from *The Cambridge Portfolio* (p. 473), No. 13 from a recent issue.

No. 14 is the inset of H. Cooke's large figure (see No. 35 in the present series, p. 43).

These last three examples are better drawn and printed than those in the years 1630, etc.

We close this series of *Cambridge Emblems and Mottoes* with a charming little impression (No. 15), measuring only 22 × 18 mm., clear cut and elegant.

No. 11

No. 12

No. 13

No. 14

No. 15

We turn to impressions of the Emblem and the Motto, of the Device and the Legend, which are enlarged by supporters or by scrolls.

And first let us take the Cambridge device (No. 16) as prefixed to Henry More's *Works* published in London by J. Macock in the year 1679; a reduced copy of which is here reproduced. (The original is 82 × 66 mm.)

This is thus described on p. 167 of Richard Ward's *Life of Henry More* (1710):

And methinks that Emblematical Representation of our Alma Mater Cantabrigia, our equally both indulgent and renown'd Mother, the University of Cambridge, with her Arms stretch'd out and Breasts flowing, holding the Sun in one Hand, and the Sacred Celestial Cup in another; with this Motto round, *Hinc Lucem et Pocula Sacra* (From whence issue Light and the Sacred Draughts of Wisdom and Knowledge) supported on both sides with the Angels, as it were, of Philosophy and Religion; I say this Noble Representation or becoming Hieroglyphick, may in a secondary sense very well befit our Author himself (as it is indeed prefix'd to his Philosophical Volumes) and be but a due Emblem of his flowing eminent Labours and Performances in the World.

No. 17 represents the device and motto supported by four Angels. It will be noticed that in the corner appears the name of *S. Gribelin*, sculp. Simon Gribelin (16611733), the line engraver, came to England c. 1680.

No. 18, with two Angel supporters, is doubtless by the same artist. It is still in use by the University Press.

No. 19, also, with two supporters, is signed S. G. (Simon Gribelin). It is rayed, as seen in the accom-panying *reduction*.

No. 20 is an interesting allegorical device, which includes the Cambridge *emblem*. The words *Spes alit Artes* surmount the whole. It is printed in the first volume of Cellarius: *Notitia Orbis Antiqui*. See Bowes's *Catalogue*, no. 356.

No. 18

No. 19

No. 20

27

The well-known figure (No. 21) of our EMBLEM, in the Map of Cambridgeshire given in Michael Drayton's *Poly-Olbion*, muſt not be omitted. The poet has two passages referring to the University, in his "One and twentieth Song":

> Then which, a purer Streame, a delicater Brooke,
> Bright Phoebus in his course, doth scarcely ouerlooke,
> Thus furniſhing her bankes; as sweetly she doth glide
> Towards Cambridge, with rich meads layd forth on either side;
> And with the Muse oft, did by the way converse: etc.

And again:

> O noble *Cambridge* then, my moſt beloved Towne,
> In glory flouriſh ſtill, to heighten thy renowne;
> The woman's perfeét shape, ſtill be thy embleme right,
> Whose one hand holds a Cup, the other bears a Light.

(At the margin of the laſt two lines are the words "The embleme of Cambridge.")

THE ARMS

THE ARMS

WE now turn to an often-repeated emblem, which combines (as seen in No. 22) the figure of Alma Mater bearing the sun and the cup, over an oval enclosing THE ARMS OF THE UNIVERSITY,* with a garter with the legend *Hinc Lucem et Pocula Sacra,* the whole supported by two robed female figures bearing palms. Underneath is a scroll with the words *Alma Mater Cantabrigia.* This combination, as stated above, is often used by the Press.

No. 23 is a somewhat similar combination, with a shield instead of an oval. It has *Alma Mater Cantabrigia* above and *Hinc Lucem et Pocula Sacra* below.

No. 24 *omits the emblem* of the *Alma Mater* and has a shield bearing THE ARMS OF THE UNIVERSITY with a flowing scroll inscribed with the motto *Hinc Lucem,* etc. This device is known at the University Press as that of Millais'.

* The University received a grant of arms: *gules a cross ermine and four gold leopards with a book gules upon the cross,* from Robert Cooke, Clarencieux King of Arms, 9 June, 1573.

No. 22

No. 23

No. 24

But here let us turn to two early Cambridge printed books which have as their device only THE ARMS OF THE UNIVERSITY.

No. 25 is from a volume printed by Thomas Thomas in the year 1584: Peter Ramus's *Dialectica Libri Duo*.

No. 26 was issued by T. and J. Buck nearly a hundred years later.

Then follows a series of devices representing the
University Arms by Mr Bruce Rogers (No. 27), by
Sir Wm St John Hope, M.A. (Peterhouse) (No. 28),
and by the late Mr J. B. Peace, M.A., of Emmanuel
College and the University Press (No. 29).

No. 30 is a flowing scroll, designed by Mr Emery
Walker, with the University Arms on a shield below.

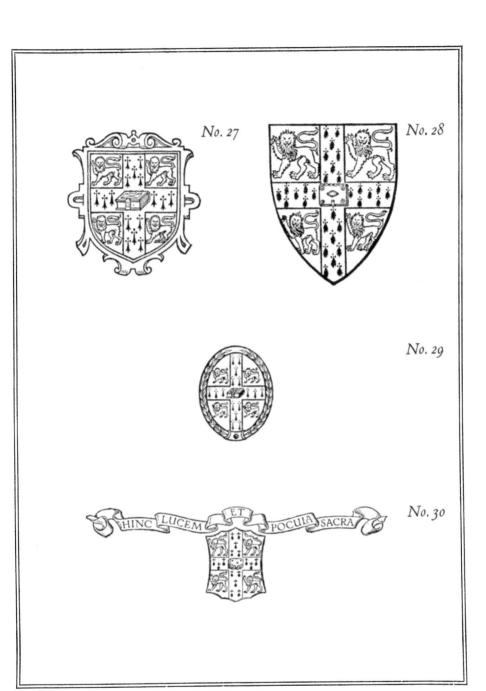

No. 27

No. 28

No. 29

No. 30

HINC LUCEM ET POCULA SACRA

No. 31 was designed by the Rev. E. E. Dorling, M.A. (Clare), for the University Press.

No. 32, by Mr George Kruger-Gray, is frequently used.

No. 31

No. 32

We may add the composite arms (No. 33) of the *Cambridge Antiquarian Society*, which, in a form similar to No. 22, has Cambridge above and Antiquarian Society below.

More frequently, however, another composite device is employed by the *C. A. S.* showing the arms of the Cambridge University, the Cambridge Town and of Ely (No. 34).

No. 33

No. 34

Laſtly, No. 35 is an elegant design, showing a robed and crowned female figure, upon whom the sun shines, while she bears a cup in one hand, the other reſting upon a book on a pedeſtal. A scroll bears the legend *Alma Mater Cantabrigia,* supported by two Angels. Below is a representation of the University and Town of Cambridge; a figure of Father Cam reclines by the river. The artiſt's name, "H. Cooke," appears in the left-hand corner.

THE MOTTO

THE MOTTO

THE first section began with a reference to the editor of *The Cambridge Portfolio* (1840), J. J. Smith, M.A., a Fellow of Gonville and Caius College. The same distinguished scholar will be recognised under his initials (J. J. S.) in the following quotation—which is taken from the first number of that useful and convenient publication *Notes and Queries*. On 1 December, 1849, we find the following question: "From what author, 'chapter and verse,' comes the Motto of the University of Cambridge, *Hinc Lucem et Pocula Sacra*? It is used as a quotation in Leighton on St Peter's Epistle; but in the last edition the learned editor does not give a reference. J. J. S."

The edition referred to is that by the Rev. J. N. Pearson (1853), who, in the *Life* of Archbishop Leighton prefixed to the first volume, quite casually quotes the Motto in the following extended form: *Hinc lucem haurire est et pocula sacra.* And in this way, indeed, the quotation is given four or five times by Leighton himself in his *Works*.

Of course the usual method of quotation is the simple form—so convenient for the legend in the garter oval—as used by the University Printer, John Legate, at the end of the 16th century: *Hinc Lucem et Pocula Sacra.*

It is ſtrange that Mr J. J. Smith, in his appeal in *Notes and Queries*, does not refer to the extended phrase, although he cannot but have noticed it. Nor does Mr Pearson comment on the words added to the ordinary Motto. Dr George Jerment also, in his edition of Leighton some years earlier, does not mark the difference. Nor again did Prof. Scholefield in his firſt issue of the *Praelectiones Theologicae*, etc., though in his second edition (1837) he printed the extended phrase in the following form: *Hinc lucem* hauriat *ac pocula sacra*; the interlineation showing that he was aware of the difference between the Cambridge Motto as usually given and the fuller quotation as printed in Leighton's *Works.*

Here it may be intereſting to notice the occasions where the archbishop quotes or refers to the phrase.

In his sermon on Psalm xxxii (Pearson's ed. ii. 21), he exclaims: "Oh, the pure, the overflowing, the in⁄comparably sweet fountain of Scripture! *Hence Light we draw and fill the Sacred Cup,*" quoting in a footnote *Hinc Lucem haurire eſt et pocula sacra.*

Again in his *Valedictory Oration* (ii. 644), Dr Leigh⁄ton says: "With regard to your reading, let it be your particular care to be familiarly acquainted with the

47

Sacred Scriptures above all other books whatever; for from thence you will truly *derive light* for your direction, and *sacred provisions* for your support on your journey."

See also the 1st Epistle of St Peter just before the end, and the *20th Theological Lecture*.

In every case it will be seen that Archbishop Leighton in his notes or in his quotations implies the fuller phrase. And yet almost invariably the shorter form of the Cambridge Motto is quoted. Even the learned Prof. J. E. B. Mayor, writing to *Notes and Queries* on 14 Oct. 1876, referring to various communications in that literary journal, says: "May I repeat the question often put, never answered—From what mediaeval poem does the Motto *Hinc lucem et pocula sacra* come?"

The quotation—given in the first section of this essay (p. 24) from Richard Ward's *Life of Henry More* (p. 167), where he translates or paraphrases the Cambridge Motto in the following words: "From whence issue Light and the Sacred Draughts of Wisdom and Knowledge"—shows that the biographer does not know the phrase in its extended form.

Prof. J. S. Reid (*Caian*, xiv. 20) says of a similar expression: "One of the many mediaeval saws, which took the form of hexameter endings, and can be assigned to no definite origin."

And again the same learned Professor wrote some time since:

In mediaeval writings there are a great many Latin verse tags, some only of which come out of known ancient literature. Some others can be traced to the abundant Latin verses poured out by Petrarca and other early Renaissance poets. This Latin poetry had immense popularity for a time, though now forgotten excepting by a scholar here and there. But it is clear that many of the tags of gnomic or proverbial character are products of the schools of the time. It is well known that teachers of grammar and logic liked to throw their maxims into verse. . . . Sometimes a tag in metrical form has been suggested by something in prose Latin literature, and it is remarkable how often (considering the times) the suggestion has even come from Greek. The date of creation of these tags is often betrayed by false quantities or barbarous grammar. . . .

However, turning from the abbreviated phrase used as the Cambridge Motto, *Hinc lucem et pocula sacra*, to the fuller quotation as given by Dr Leighton, *Hinc lucem haurire est et pocula sacra*, we see that we are not dealing with a mere Latin tag.* And this especially when we notice the full English translation given by the archbishop in his comments on the 32nd Psalm. This is how he gives it: "Hence Light *we draw* and *fill* the Sacred Cup."

* The late Public Orator (Sir John Sandys), who at one time regarded the Motto as a mere tag, but afterwards recognised the hexameter, once sent to the present writer a list of the occasions on which he used the usual phrase in his official speeches. It will be seen, from his *Orationes et Epistolae Cantabrigienses* (1910), that in his first oration, on 30 Nov. 1876, he aptly introduced part of the phrase.

This suggests that *the full hexameter line* may be

HINC LUCEM HAURIRE EST ET POCULA
SACRA REPLERE.

Prof. Reid writing of this says: "I think that the presence of the word *haurire* affords no indication of date or source. *Haurire lucem* is good Latin at all periods of the language." Again the same scholar writes: "One point makes me think that the metrical phrase has a rather late origin. It is, that in late Latin *pocula* occurs very frequently in the sense of a noxious, especially a magical potion. The epithet *sacra* seems to have been put in expressly to counteract that common use."

But though we have perhaps recovered the hexameter, the poem and its author are still to seek.

APPENDIX

APPENDIX

No. 36. The University Emblem, with the full motto.

No. 37. The Arms of the University, with the full motto.

No. 36

No. 37

PRINTED
BY
WALTER  LEWIS, M.A.
AT
THE CAMBRIDGE
UNIVERSITY
PRESS

www.ingramcontent.com/pod-product-compliance
Ingram Content Group UK Ltd.
Pitfield, Milton Keynes, MK11 3LW, UK
UKHW042156280225
455719UK00001B/368